FIDEL CASTRO El Líder Máximo: A Life in Pictures

El Líder Máximo: A Life in Pictures El Líder Máximo: A Life in Pictures

WHITE STAR PUBLISHERS

FIDEL CASTRO

Máximo: A Life in Pictures El Líder Máximo: A Life in Pictures El Líder Máximo: A Life in Pictures

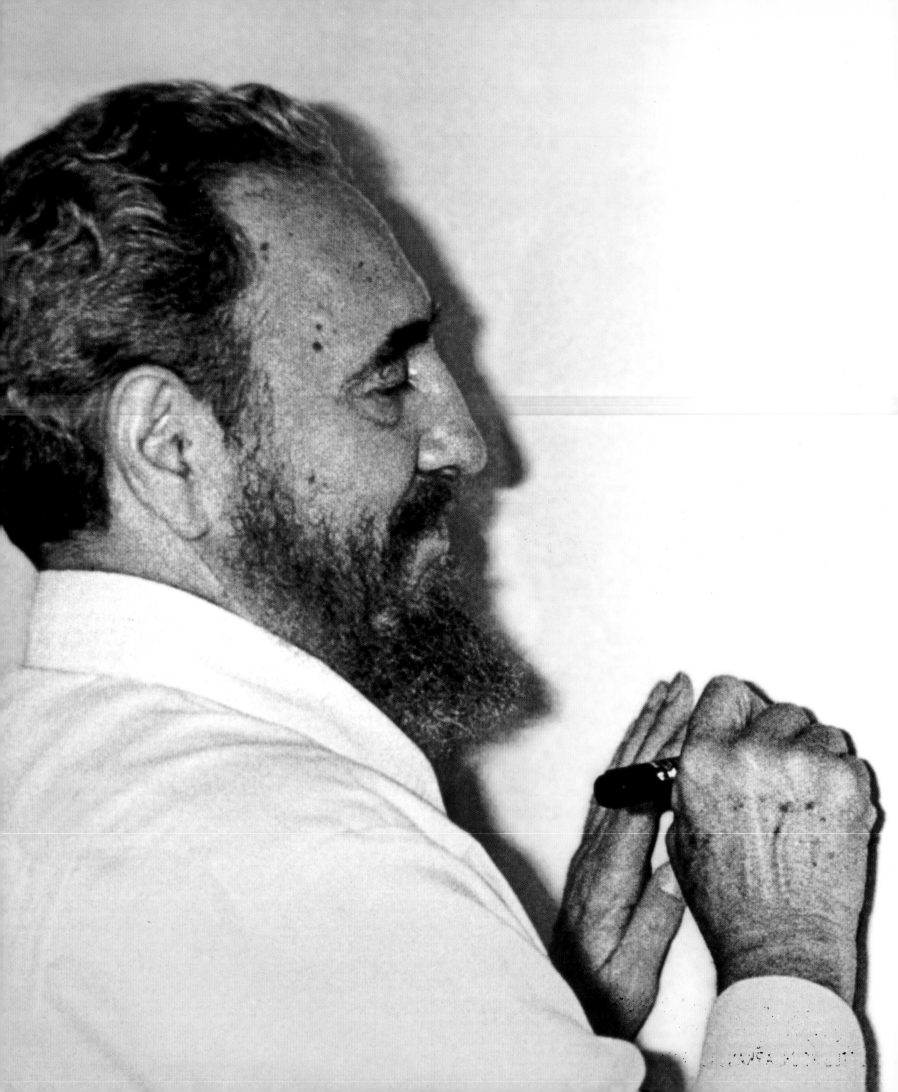

EDITED BY
VALERIA MANFERTO DE FABIANIS

TEXT
LUCIANO GARIBALDI

GRAPHIC LAYOUT
PATRIZIA BALOCCO LOVISETTI

© 2007 White Star s.p.a.
Via Candido Sassone, 22/24
13100 Vercelli, Italy
www.whitestar.it

TRANSLATION TEXT: DAVIDE ARNOLD LAMAGNI
TRANSLATION CAPTIONS: GLENN DEBATTISTA

ISBN: 978-88-544-0340-6

REPRINTS:
1 2 3 4 5 6   11 10 09 08 07

Color separation: Fotomec, Turin
Printed in China

3 A young student attending the Jesuit school of Santiago de Cuba in Havana, Fidel Castro proves himself an intelligent and determined boy.

4 Castro photographed one of his meetings, his unmistakable profile traced by floodlight.

6 The líder maximo signs on a panel during a public manifestation in Havana in the 80's.

10-11 A famous photograph of Castro with his comrades of many battles: Ernesto "Che" Guevara, and the inseparable cigar in his mouth.

Contents

"He has the almost mystical conviction

that the best achievement for a human

being is the good formation of his conscience

and that, moral stimuli, more than material ones,

are capable of changing the world and of inducing

history. I think he is one of the great idealists

of our time and that this, perhaps,

may be his greatest virtue, even

if for him it has also been

his greatest danger."

Gabriel Garcia Márquez

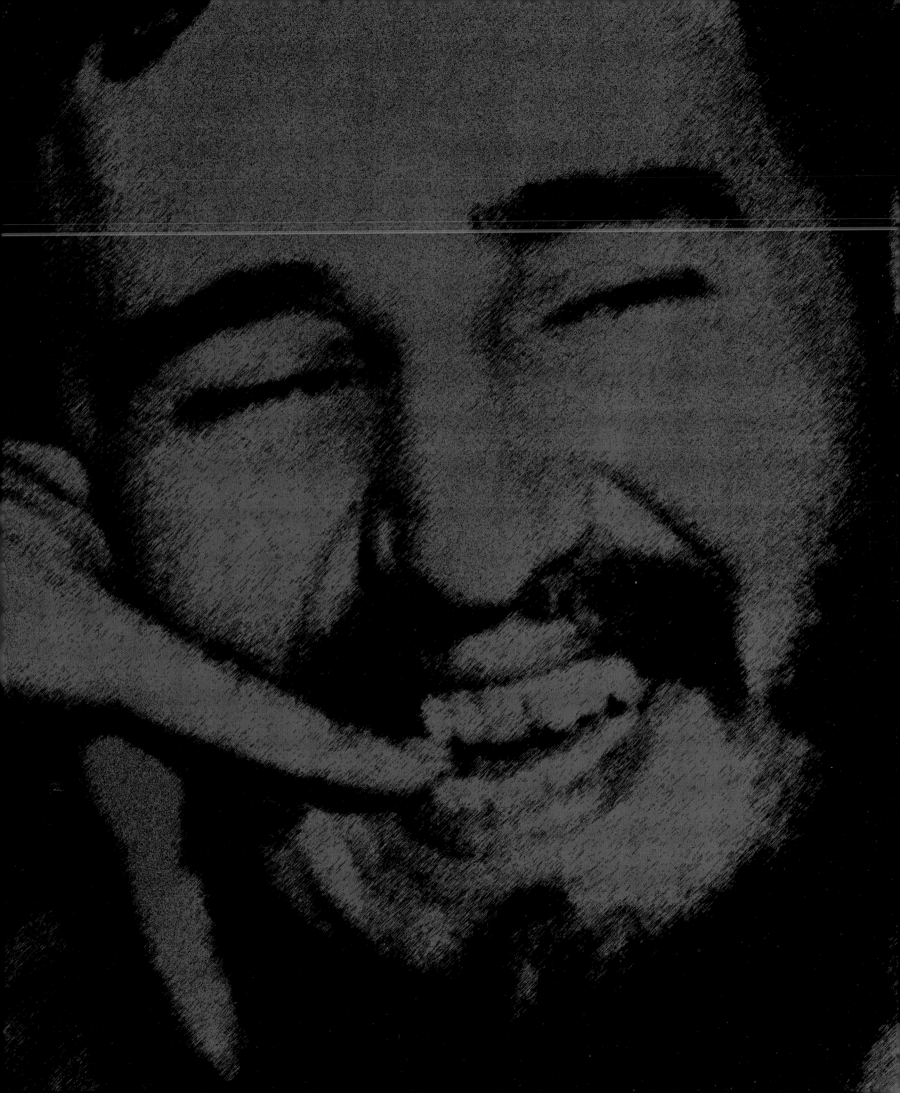

FIDEL CASTRO

El Líder Máximo: A Life in Pictures

INTRODUCTION

FIDEL CASTRO LIDER MAXIMO

If Fulgencio Batista (1901-1973) had not existed, Cuba and the world would never have had a revolutionary and a dictator of the caliber of Fidel Castro. His spirit of revolt, his warrior's impetus and his will to destroy a hateful and hated dictatorship distinguished the young Fidel Castro from his very first moves in the political arena. The ex-army sergeant, Batista, had in fact, in 1933 at just 32 years of age, helped overthrow the dictator Gerardo Machado. Immediately afterwards, with a handful of violent and unscrupulous militiamen, he overthrew the provisional government of Carlos Manuel de Céspedes. Self-proclaiming himself Army Chief of Staff, Batista set up and controlled a series of puppet presidents until 1940, when he got himself elected in a totally manipulated election. Thus, as President of the Republic, he participated, though only symbolically, in the Second World War, an ally of the United States. This earned him credit internationally, credit which he would otherwise never have received.

One of Cuba's recurring economic crises, worsened by Batista's greed and unscrupulousness, led him to resign in 1944 and retire to his golden refuge in Florida. Then, in 1952, he again took control by force, overthrowing the government of Carlos Prío Socarrás and canceling the forthcoming parliamentary elections, one of whose candidates was a young lawyer called Fidel Castro, the 26-year-old leader of the "Orthodox Party" (as we will see, Fidel reacted to this illegality with the legendary assault on the Moncada Barracks on July 26th, 1953). Afterwards, according a well-rehearsed plan, Batista 'won' the general elections of 1954, then those of 1958. The regime was to crumble when the United States, tired of protecting and financing the dictator-president, ended all arms supplies to Cuba. The American government never even for a moment imagined that, by doing so, it had opened the way to the worst enemy they could imagine.

Having put the Fidel myth's historical origins into context we will take short panoramic glance at the human and political progress of our subject island. Cuba, with its 10 million inhabitants, of whom 70 percent are white, is the biggest island in the Antilles. At its widest point, it is 683 miles (1100 km) across. Cuba is the world's biggest producer of sugar cane (over 60 million tons per year), and is a major producer of coffee and cereal. Havana cigars, of which more than 200 million are made annually, are the world's most appreciated. Cuba also has petroleum, natural gas and sulfur. Its independence from Spain dates back to 1898, following the end of the Spanish-American war. After the end of that conflict, Cuba remained under U.S.A. military administration until 1902 and then again from 1906 to 1910. Today, Guantánamo – which hosts the controversial prison for Muslim terrorists captured in Iraq and Afghanistan – remains an American military base on Cuban territory.

On this island, in the village of Birán, in the province Holguín, on 13 August 1926 Fidel Castro came to the world. He was the third child of Angel Castro and Lina Ruz González, well-to-do farmers and owners of a large holding about 18 miles (30 km) from the sea. Angel was Spanish, born in Galicia. He arrived in Cuba with the Spanish troops at the time of the Spanish-American war. He had had five children by his first wife, Maria Luisa Argota Reyes. Then she had left him and Angel fell for the very young Lina Ruz, whom he was to marry as his second wife. She gave him five children, in order: Angelita, Rámon, Fidel, Raúl (destined, at a young age, to succeed his brother as first citizen of the country), and Emma.

As the children of a woman with deep Catholic feelings, the young Castros received a faith-based education from the Jesuits. They first attended the La Salle and the Dolores colleges of Santiago, then the renowned Belén College, run by the Havana Jesuits. It is impossible to reconstruct how, where and when the dissident and revolutionary ideas that were destined to shape young Fidel's destiny were born within him. Perhaps it was a tutor concerned to help the weaker classes; this would not have been unusual. The fact remains that at the beginning of 1940, when just 13 years of age, Fidel tried to organize a sugar workers' strike – even though it was damaging of his own father. The reason? The workers weren't paid enough. The responsibility, in the young Fidel's mind resided less with his unfortunate father than with the exploitive American-owned United Fruit Company, to which Angel Castro sold the produce of his land.

The young Fidel already bore the traces of the personality that many years later the Nobel Prize laureate Gabriel Garcia Márquez described with these words "The Fidel Castro I think I know is a man of austere customs and insatiable illusions, with a formal and old-fashioned education of weighted words and delicate manners, incapable of conceiving an idea which is not extraordinary. . . . He has the almost mystical conviction that the best outcome of a human being is through a good education of his conscience, and that moral stimuli, more than material ones, are capable of changing the world and driving history. I believe he is one of the great idealists of our time, and that this may be his best quality, even if for him it has been his biggest danger."

After finishing school at 19, Castro enrolled in the Law Faculty of the University of Havana. But did he really want to be a lawyer? In an interview, regarding this choice, he once said, "I ask myself why I chose Law. I don't know. I put it partly down to the habit of discussing and arguing. That's how I convinced myself that I was fit for advocacy." In fact, as we will see, words were never to fail him and he has always been an extraordinary orator. The university was for him also a place in which to become passionately engaged in politics. He in fact soon became part of a student organization protesting against the regime which was at the time not that of the tyrannical and bloodthirsty Fulgencio Batista (who abandoned power in 1944 and took it back in 1952), but one which was certainly managerial and would not tolerate violent opposition. His first "political act," which took place on February 12th, 1948 as the organizer and leader of a student uprising against the police was sparked by the desire to assert the autonomy of the University and other state institutes. It was the right occasion for Fidel to test his grit.

Only two months later Castro was in Bogotá, the capital of Colombia, leading a march of Cuban and Argentine students who had gone there to demonstrate against the planned Pan-American conference which was to found the O.S.A. – the Organization of American States, inspired by the collaboration principles of the United States. The American government in fact sent General Marshall to Bogotá (he had been an architect of victory in WWII), who was considered to be the 'patron' of the new alliance. It was an initiative that certainly not did not go down well with the communist world. There are those in the U.S.A. who even who accuses the Soviet secret services of having financed the Argentine-Cuban student protest.

Thousands of flyers were distributed on the roads to Bogotá, accusing the United States of hoping to "colonize"

Central and Southern America. Shops were looted, police stations assaulted, and cars set on fire. It was an anticipation of what was to happen much later, all over Europe, on the occasion of the various world summits (G8 nations, etc.). General Marshall attributed the responsibility for the disorders to the communists, and the government-aligned press named Fidel Castro as the organizer and leader of the protest. No-one, though, was able to arrest him. The future lawyer Castro returned to Havana and married his girlfriend, Mirta Díaz Balart, sister of Rafael, a childhood friend and a university companion. They were divorced each other just six years later, and Mirta settled in the United States, leaving her ex-husband with their son. He was also named Fidel, and was called "Fidelito." He became a nuclear physicist in the U.S.S.R.

Soon after the marriage, celebrated on 12 October 1948, Rafael, Fidel's brother-in-law, began to support the party of the exiled Fulgencio Batista, with a view to bringing about his return to power. Castro was no longer unknown. His name featured in the newspapers and in political circles as that of a fierce revolutionary. Rafael arranged a meeting between the two: he was hoping to convince Fidel to end his anti-capitalistic attitudes and support Batista, who had, among much else, all the financial resources needed. This proved a wasted effort. Fidel had made his choice: a friend of Russia; an enemy of the U.S.A.

Castro graduated in law in 1950 and became a junior lawyer in a small practice. But he had politics on his mind, not the legal profession. "I had read the 'Manifesto of the Communist Party' by Karl Marx and Friedrich Engels and Lenin's writings," he was to say, "and I was already profoundly influenced by Marxism."

Years of intense activity followed: meetings, conventions, forming various communist sections in various centers of the country, attacking the large landowners and especially the United States and its "imperialism." During this period, Fulgencio Batista returned to Cuba and overthrew the legitimate government, replacing it with a new military dictatorship. Castro reacted with force, denouncing Batista to the authorities for violation of the Constitution, but his appeal was rejected.

A fatal decision. The young revolutionary, in fact, did not take the defeat too well and reacted by taking up arms and organizing, with his companions, the armed assault of the Moncada Barracks in Santiago. His aim was to take control of the arsenal and offer a show of power against the reinstated dictator. July 26th, 1953 was the fateful date. Castro and his comrades attacked at dawn. But the barracks immediately responded, returning vigorous fire. Perhaps

an informer had infiltrated Castro's group. Bloodshed followed. The survivors, about seventy persons, mostly students, were taken prisoner, tortured and nearly all executed on the spot. But Fidel was spared. Injured and tortured, he was jailed in the Isle of Pines prison, to await a trial which was generally expected to end with a death sentence. But things went differently.

The hearings began in December. Castro was allowed to represent himself and made a speech which was to become famous. Perhaps he had sensed that he was not going to be given the death sentence. He might have been told that the archbishop of Havana was moving to save from execution an ex-Jesuit schoolboy whose parents were closely linked to the Church. At the end of a very harsh attack lasting hours, against capitalism, exploitation and the Western warmongering tendencies, he concluded with these words "I know well that imprisonment will be hard for me, but it has always been so for anyone else, full of vile threats and horrible tortures. But I am not afraid of prison, as I am not afraid of the wrath of that miserable tyrant who ended the lives of seventy of my brothers. Condemn me, I don't care. History will absolve me." His companions in chains looked at him, perplexed and incredulous. He was sentenced to 15 years of jail. Upon his release, following an amnesty in 1955, Castro went in exile to Mexico.

In that same year, in political refugee circles in Mexico City, he met Ernesto Guevara, a young Argentine doctor who had also escaped from a country in which he could not see himself living anymore. The impact was immediate and total. At the end of the encounter, Guevara had become totally passionate about Castro's beliefs and said to him and his comrades, "From now one, call me 'Che.'" The word "che," in the Guaraní dialect which Guevara had spoken since he was a boy, means "mine." His meaning was: "Consider me yours," and it forged a bond that was to remain unbroken until Guevara's death. In turn, Fidel Castro enrolled Guevara as a physician in the "26th of July Movement," which was so-named to commemorate the sacrifice of the assault on Moncada Barracks, and which hoped at some future time to launch an expedition against Fulgencio Batista.

Following a tip-off, the Mexican police arrested the entire exile group. Two months later, in August 1956, they were released. It was said that "someone" had posted the huge bail the judges had set for the prisoners' provisional release; it was further hinted that Mexico's ex-president Lázaro Cárdenas was involved in the matter. The newly found freedom put the fire in the "movement." Castro got hold of a boat which was renamed *Granma* ("Grandmother"). The yacht, with the word "freedom" onto the flag, left Mexico late at night on November 24th, 1956 from the port of Tuxpan, with 82 armed men who had been trained on the farm of an ex-militiaman of Pancho Villa's. A terrible storm was taking place. The crossing was dramatic from every point of view. Few of the men were mariners. It took them a good seven days to reach their destination. They disembarked at dawn on December 2nd on Playa de las Coloradas. In Mexico City the newspapers reported that the men were thought to have drowned.

Everyone know of the enterprise; it strongly reminded them, on a smaller scale, of that of The Thousand, that had occurred nearly a century earlier. But things didn't go that way. On that stormy beach, "Che" met Camilo Cienfuegos, who was there waiting for Castro and his companions. He became his best friend, and together, the young revolutionaries began their march in the Sierra Maestra. They weren't to have much breathing room. Batista's army, quickly mobilized and made up of fierce soldiers, used to tearing flesh off prisoners with red hot pliers, dispersed the expedition, killing nearly all of its members. Castro with eleven men, among whom were his brother Raúl, Che and Camilo Cienfuegos, managed to survive and began their guerilla war. After a 20-hour march, they  reached the peaks of the Sierra Maestra. The group of survivors grew quickly to an 800-strong squadron. *Campesinos*, farm hands, miners and also students kept arriving to join the 'movement.' They became the *barbudos* (the bearded men), having sworn not to shave until the island was liberated. For over two years, throughout 1957 and 1958, fighting went on in the Sierra, through famine and disease, continuous clashes with the army and ferocious attacks on police barracks. The battles of El Hombuto (August 30th, 1957) and Pino del Agua (September 16th, 1957) were particularly bloody.

Batista had organized a force of 10,000 men armed to the teeth, but Castro had the farmers and laborers on his side and managed to inflict heavy losses on the enemy. On October 26th, 1958 he competed a tactical maneuver which allowed him to split the island Cuba in two, establishing an unassailable line of defense after having captured the Guinia Barracks, in Miranda. On December 28th, 1958 the forced led by Che occupied Santa Clara, in the heart of Cuba. The day after, they derailed a train with 408 of Batista's soldiers on board: it was a massacre.

On 1 January 1st, 1959 the column led by Che entered Havana, occupying the La Cabaña military fort. Victory was upon them. Batista escaped, first to the Dominican Republic, then to Portugal with an undisclosed number of suitcases full of gold. From there he went to Franco's Spain, where he died of a natural causes in 1973.

20 Taken from a commemorative picture, in this panel, Fidel and Camilo Cienfuegos, the revolutionary chief killed during the battles for the conquest of power, stand with the "Granma" as backdrop, the yacht with which Castro and his "rebels" disembarked in Cuba on December 2nd, 1956.

21 Left, Fidel Castro and "Che" Guevara discuss in Sierra Maestra where a fierce battle has been going for over two years to destroy Fulgencio Batista's dictatorship. Right, the Líder talks with his brother Raúl (close up) and other guerillas.

On 8 January 1959, Fidel Castro solemnly entered the capital, leading his army. The day after he proclaimed himself Prime Minister and nominated Manuel Urrutia Lleó president of the Republic. After two months he went on a visit to New York where he was welcomed triumphantly. The crowd applauded him like a hero. A group of Italian descent, thinking they would please him, gave him the Fascist salute. Castro responded readily "My model is Garibaldi, not Mussolini."

They had promised they would shave once they had conquered the island, but Castro never shaved and didn't want to demobilize. Cuba needed patient work of economic and social reconstruction. Fidel instead let success get the better of him. When he was still a student of the Jesuits, a teacher of his had written about him "Theatrical characteristics, could do well in acting." An accurate picture of his character. He would exalt himself in pompous four-hour speeches. He nationalized and expropriated everything possible, heavily intervening in families' private business and the freedom of citizens. Some significant examples: rents decreased by 50 percent, with the transformation of lodgers into real owners through a forced purchase with monthly installments proportional to their earnings; he closed the casinos; expropriated hotels, beaches and private clubs; he introduced a limit on agricultural property of 990 acres (400 hectares): the excess was 'nationalized,' i.e., requisitioned by the State; he abolished trade unions, holding them to be 'useless'; he closed newspapers and ended the freedom of the press.

At the same time, the squaring up was taking place with Batista's 'fascists.' Che Guevara was entrusted with this task, 'supreme judge' with additional powers for the prevention of a possible and feared 'counterrevolution.' In fact, there were some counterrevolutionaries and every now and then they turned up in nighttime shoot-outs. Once caught, they were generally regularly tried and even had defense lawyers. The latter rarely managed to save their clients from being executed, though. Hundreds of policemen, accused of war crimes including the torture and murder of prisoners, were shot. Many high-level officers were exiled, though not Fidel Castro's brother-in-law, who had become a minister in the last Batista government.

In the first weeks after having taken power, Castro and the movement, by then openly communist, began to upset the farmers with his program nationalizing plantations. Here is a passage from the eloquent letter which Fidel's mother, Lina Ruz Gonzáles, sent her son (joking, but up to a point): "If you dare nationalize our plantations, then I will wait

22 The "Commander" makes his triumphant entry to Havana – already conquered by his men – on January 8th, 1959. The civil war is over. Batista the dictator has escaped, taking with him a stolen gold of inestimable worth, and the crowd awards a huge welcome to the man who, from this moment, will govern Cuba for 48 years.

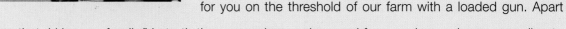

for you on the threshold of our farm with a loaded gun. Apart from that, I kiss you fondly." In truth the *campesinos*, colons and farm workers, whom, according to Castro, would have become free from a secular misery by becoming owners, were worse off than before. The real owners, now expelled by the new regime, had at least paid them. But Castro did not have any money for the farmers. To the contrary, quite soon the rationing of basic foods occurred: meat, eggs, milk, butter and bread.

In the meantime, the Marxist-Leninist wholesale land expropriation program and state management of agricultural production wasn't producing results, and discontent over the "betrayed revolution" grew in pace with the repression, which often caught up those who had fought next to Castro. Escapes into exile began, most to the United States.

By getting rid of all foreign companies – starting with the sugar producers – whose property was confiscated without any compensation, he put production into even more treacherous hands, usually inexperienced and incapable ones. The result was that production fell to the lowest levels in history, while export markets (the primary one being the U.S.) refused Cuban products. The consequences were unemployment, unhappiness, and hunger.

At that point Castro sought help beyond the Iron Curtain, becoming a flag bearer for world communism, and at the same time an instrument of the U.S.S.R. Che Guevara was assigned the task of making contact with Moscow and satellite countries. On 15 February 1960 meetings began with Anastas Mikoyan, Soviet Vice Prime Minister. These concluded with a grandiose nearly 10,000 sq. ft (9000 sq. m) exposition organized in Havana to present the U.S.S.R.'s scientific progress. At the end of this the two countries signed a five-year agreement thanks to which Cuba was able to buy Soviet goods, especially petroleum, at a price 33 percent below U.S. prices. In exchange, Cuba supplied 1 million metric tons of sugar per year at a price above that of the international market. Russia also supplied Cuba with arms, technical and military assistance and a credit of $100 million, to be paid back over 12 years at an annual interest rate of 2.5 percent. A Soviet oil tanker, the *Beijing* was to be the first to ship to Cuba the oil the United States had denied. Meetings in China followed, with Zhou Enlai and Mao Zedong, with whom "Che" signed a treaty covering economic cooperation, scientific and technical aid. The road was by then open to the whole communist world and Cuba signed advantageous agreements with the Democratic Republic of Korea, Czechoslovakia, the German Democratic Republic, and one by one with all of Moscow's satellite states.

24 Left, Fidel embraces the Soviet leader Khrushchev at the United Nations of New York in September 1960.

Right, Castro talks with landowners to explain their importance in the agrarian reform which started in 1960.

There's no such thing as a free lunch. It is true that the Soviet payback for such a generous policy with Cuba came soon, with Castro allowing Khrushchev to install an impressive series of mid-range nuclear missile bases, with the missiles aimed at the United States. American reconnaissance planes soon spotted and photographed the launch sites. The news was made public amid much clamor. The supreme command of the U.S. Army suggested to John F. Kennedy that he authorize out a surprise large-scale attack on Cuba, but the president did not feel like throwing the country into a war with unpredictable escalation consequences.

A bold initiative like the Russian-Cuban one could not be left unanswered and it soon became the world's hottest political topic. For the United States, the Soviet missiles were an intolerable provocation: a point of no-return in the Cold War which had lasted since the end of WWII with Stalin's decision to divide Europe in two, raising what Winston Churchill, in his famous Fulton speech, had termed "the Iron Curtain." In the United States there was in fact an authentic mobilization against Cuba. Many Cuban exiles who had left the island after being deprived of their lands and their homes decided to take arms and enrolled as mercenaries to settle up with Castro once and for all. A real expedition corps was formed: 1500 volunteers who disembarked in several groups on April 1st, 1961, on the Bahia de Cochinos – the "Bay of Pigs." The declared intent was to dismantle the Soviet missile silos. But the enterprise was destined to fail. Intercepted by Castro's helicopters, the expedition became a bloodbath. While survivors were being imprisoned and sentenced to death, demonstrations were held all over South America in favor of Cuba and against the United States, accused the latter of having financed and organized the attack. Kennedy did not back down. He admitted the responsibility of the U.S. secret services for the initiative, holding that he had every right to help the volunteers in the interests of the country and announced the ending of diplomatic relations with Cuba and the total embargo against the island. All NATO states followed him and so did Latin America nations, except for Mexico.

The situation was about to explode, with the risk of a war breaking out between Cuba and the United States. On October 22nd, 1962, concluding a crescendo of verbal violence and ever heavier threats, Kennedy decreed a naval blockade against Cuba (no vessel could either approach or leave the island) and asked the Soviet Union for the immediate withdrawal of the strategic missiles. At this point the world trembled: a third world war, not a local war, seemed to be about to break. Pope John XXIII intervened, imploring Khrushchev and Kennedy to recommence dia-

logue and save the world from horrendous bloodshed, which, given the atomic weapons of the great powers, would have been unprecedented.

History tells us that Khrushchev took the first step, ordering his ships heading for Cuba to do an about-turn and, keeping Castro, decided to attack diplomatically. Finally, the Russian leader gave orders to have the missile stations dismantled. Kennedy also responded. As soon as aerial reconnaissance informed him that the dismantling had begun, he ordered the war ships patrolling Cuban waters return to port, and thus lifted the blockade. He also declared that the United States would not instigate uprisings or coups against Cuba.

In as far as regards the Catholic Church, the ex-Jesuit scholar expressed no gratitude to the Pope who had contributed so much to sparing Cuba potential bloodshed. In fact, relations had been tense for quite a while already. In May 1961 Castro had already ordered the closing of all religious colleges and had confiscated their sites. On September 17th of the same year, Cuba expelled 131 Catholic priests and monks accused of plotting against "el pueblo." Finally, on January 3rd, 1961, Pope John XXIII excommunicated Castro in keeping with the pontifical decree of 1949 with which Pius XII had forbidden Catholics, upon the penalty of excommunication, to support communist governments and parties.

Between the end of April and early May 1963 Fidel Castro carried out his first official visit to the U.S.S.R., triumphantly acclaimed by the crowds mobilized by the authorities. He brought home a highly positive result: Khrushchev had agreed to buying Cuba's entire sugar production at a price very advantageous for Cuba. Castro thanked him, and upon his return to Cuba he instituted military service. The following year he went on a second trip to Moscow. Once back in Havana, he organized the first Congress of Latin-American Communists. It was all too easy for his opponents who had found refuge in the United States to accuse him of having become a pawn of the U.S.S.R. In fact, Cuba had become the platform of Moscow in the heart of the American continent. On that same year the Cuban Communist Party came to life.

26 In October 22nd 1962, following

the discovery of Soviet missiles

installed on the island, American

president John F. Kennedy

announces to the world, two days

later, a total embargo of man

and merchandise against

the island of Cuba.

The Soviets returned the visits and in 1965 a crowded delegation arrived led by Russia's Foreign Minister, Andrei Gromyko. Soon afterwards, Che Guevara began his missions to Africa, where he had rushed with about a hundred volunteers to organize the resistance against U.S.-supported Moise Tshombe, who had taken power in Congo ousting Patrice Lumumba. It was only the first of a series of international military expeditions financed by the KGB, which were to extend to Guinea-Bissau, the Cape Verde Islands, and Angola, before starting uprisings in Latin America.

Castro defined 1966 as 'the year of solidarity.' In Havana he convoked the "Tri-continental Conference" to give life to the project of exporting the Cuban communist revolution. Around one table sat all the revolutionaries of Africa, Asia and Latin America. It was solemnly proclaimed "the right of peoples to respond with revolutionary violence to imperialist violence." It was a response to a resolution which had been adopted shortly before by the House of Representatives of Washington which said that the United States reserved the "right to intervene with arms in any Latin-American country so as to prevent subversive activities."

The decision of the Cuba summit led to a lot of protest even inside the communist world, between the hardliners (supporting Cuba) and the supporters of a legal political opposition. Castro launched hard and bitter accusations against those communist parties that had rejected the principle of the armed struggle. In particular, Venezuela and China bore the brunt, the latter for its refusal to supply Cuba with low-cost rice.

On October 9th, 1967 Che Guevara, caught the previous day by Bolivian government agents (with whom CIA agents were collaborating), was assassinated in a place called Valle Grande. Before being thrown into a mass grave, from which he was exhumed twenty years later, his body was photographed and the dramatic image of the great revolutionary lying on a stone slab was seen the world over.

27 Ernesto "Che" Guevara, whose
body is shown here surrounded by
soldiers and by Bolivian agents, was
executed in October 1967. Guevara
had the mission of fomenting
a Communist revolution in Bolivia.

It was the definitive failure of the project of exporting the revolution on a planetary scale. His last message sent to the Organization for the Solidarity of the People of Africa, Asia and Latin America (OSPAAAL) concluded with this exhortation: "10, 100, 1000 Vietnams!"

After Che's death Cuba experienced a long period of ups and downs. On the one hand, Castro began to take some genuinely positive initiatives, such as the mass literacy campaign, with 270,000 teachers and students successfully mobilized. Child death rates were reduced, as confirmed by WHO (the World Health Organization), and tourism was increased in every way, making of Cuba the second most popular tourist resort in the Caribbean after the Dominican Republic. Toward the end of the 1980s the flow of money from Cubans who had become US citizens and sent money to their families and friends was estimated at $850 million per year. These positive aspects of the Castro dictatorship led to more than one western intellectual to speak in favor of the regime. One has only to recall the two documentary interviews with Fidel made by the famous U.S. director Oliver Stone ("Comandante," 2003 and "Looking for Fidel," 2004).

On the other hand there are quite a few violations of human rights – censorship, to the total absence of freedom of the press, the absurd need to have a special authorization (not from the police but from the Communist Party) to connect to the Internet, plus crimes such as the sinking of the boat *13 de Marzo* which, with 71 escaping Cubans, was trying to reach Florida. This occurred on the morning of July 13th, 1994. Surrounded by coast guard interceptors, even before reaching international waters, the refugees were wiped out by machine-gun fire. A total of 41 died, including women and children; the survivors were imprisoned.

In March 2003 one of the many raids the police force's political teams organized rounded up and jailed 75 independent journalists and human rights activists. At the conclusion of their trials, they all received 28-year sentences. The organization "Reporters Without Borders" has classified Cuba as being in sec-

28 Left, with Elian Gonzáles'
grandfather, a myth for the Cubans.
Right, with John Paul II during his
visit to Cuba in 1997.

ond to last place in freedom of the press, out of 167 countries. Amnesty International has repeatedly condemned the Castro regime: since 1988 the organization has been barred from Cuban territory.

To be fair, one must also remember the acts of terrorism perpetrated by some Cuban exiles to revenge the wrongs of the regime. Among them is the 1976 attack against a "Cubana de Aviación" plane in which 73 people died, and the bomb detonated by Luis Posada Carriles in 1997 at the Hotel Copacabana. He himself claimed responsibility for the incident in an interview with the *New York Times* in July 1998, justifying it as an attempt at causing a crisis for Cuba's tourist industry. Among the armed attacks of U.S. origin one must recall the American invasion of Grenada in 1983. On this island in the Lesser Antilles, a military clique supported by Cuba had taken power and Castro-minded elements had occupied public buildings and barracks. Washington mobilized units of the U.S. Marine Corps, which landed on the island and defeated the Cuban contingent in short time. President Ronald Reagan justified the attack without mincing words "We went to Grenada not to defend someone else's interests, but our own. Because now our interests have a global nature and should be defended in any part of the world where they are threatened."

The ideological rigor of Castroism was weakened (and it could nor have been otherwise) by the fall of the Berlin wall and the implosion of the U.S.S.R. in 1989. Khrushchev's Moscow, then Brezhnev's until 1985, when Mikhail Gorbachov became secretary-general of the Communist Party, started distancing the U.S.S.R. from Cuba, although they had always been the regime's great protector and had supported its wobbly economy with a lot of money. With decreased support from the 'parent company' Cuba had to undertake a challenging road toward integration – both political and economic – in the world arena. In this situation, Castro found unexpected and providential help from Pope John Paul II, ready to receive him in the Vatican in 1996, during his trip to Italy. The visit was returned in 1997, with an unexpected and strong criticism of the American embargo. Castro made a series of openings toward the Cuban Catholic Church and eased tensions with the United States. The confirmation was the words of solidarity for the U.S.A. which Castro pronounced on the occasion of the Twin Tower attacks of September 11th, 2001, words which were returned with the authorization by Washington for the export to Cuba of food and pharmaceutical products.

30 Born in August 13th, 1926, at the threshold of turning 80, Fidel is struck by illness which forces him on July 31st 2006 to transfer power to his brother Raúl, 5 years younger.

Late on the morning of August 1st, 2006 all Cuban TV and radio programs were interrupted to broadcast a government message: President Fidel Castro had been rushed to Havana's main hospital, suffering from a gastrointestinal hemorrhage. Leadership of the nation devolved upon Castro's brother Raúl, 75, who served as defense minister. Fidel was to undergo a surgical operation on his colon.

Some wept, some celebrated. On August 13th, Castro turned 80. Celebrations had been planned well ahead. They were all cancelled. What has become of him? Official sources are quiet. Could he be already dead? On October 30th, after a month of total absence from the TV screens, Castro returned on video in the course of a program broadcast from the hospital to which he had been taken. He made this appearance to quell all insinuations about his health and status. On November 12th, U.S.A. sources spread the news that "el líder máximo" was very ill. He was said to have cancer of the colon that had reached a terminal state, with a metastasis in the stomach. One month later, on December 15th, John Negroponte, head of the CIA, added more "He is about to die," he told the *Washington Post*. The answer arrived on 30 December, when Castro read a message to the nation on the occasion of the New Year: "My slow road to recovery is all but completed."

Since then catastrophic announcements and denials have alternated. Concurrently, Raúl Castro was taking things one step at a time. Born in June 1931, Raúl was, together with Fidel and Che Guevara and Camilo Cienfuegos (who died fighting), one of the four of the march on Havana. Always at Fidel's side since that tragic July 26th, 1953, the day of the abortive assault on the Moncada Barracks, he was nominated Minister of Defense, taking power on January 1st, 1959, and then, in 1964, became Secretary of the Central Committee of the Cuban Communist Party. In the few months in which he has had executive power, he has (though certainly in strict agreement with his brother) proven moderate and open to unhoped-for openings toward the historical enemy of the U.S.A. It is of course the same U.S.A. in which Alina Fernández Revuelta, the illegitimate and secret daughter of Fidel lives in exile in Washington, working as a CNN journalist. Alina Fernández Revuelta was born in 1956 from a relationship between the dictator and Natalia Revuelta, and escaped from Cuba in 1993 using false identity papers. Alina has always been a bitter enemy of her father's. One recalls her well-known reports in which she denounces the crimes committed by the *barbudos* and the terrible conditions in which political prisoners in Cuba were forced to live. After Castro's withdrawal from the political scene because of the illness, Alina gave an interview to Alessandra Farkas, in which she asserts that Fidel, following his illness, has "rediscovered Jesus upon his deathbed and it doesn't surprise me that much because he was education was from the Jesuits. I think he is now more interested in the fate of his soul than the future of Cuba. But I think that his final face-off will be with history. Some books will speak of him as a hero, leader and revolutionary. Others as a cruel and bloodthirsty dictator. Even after his death, he will continue dividing and causing arguments."

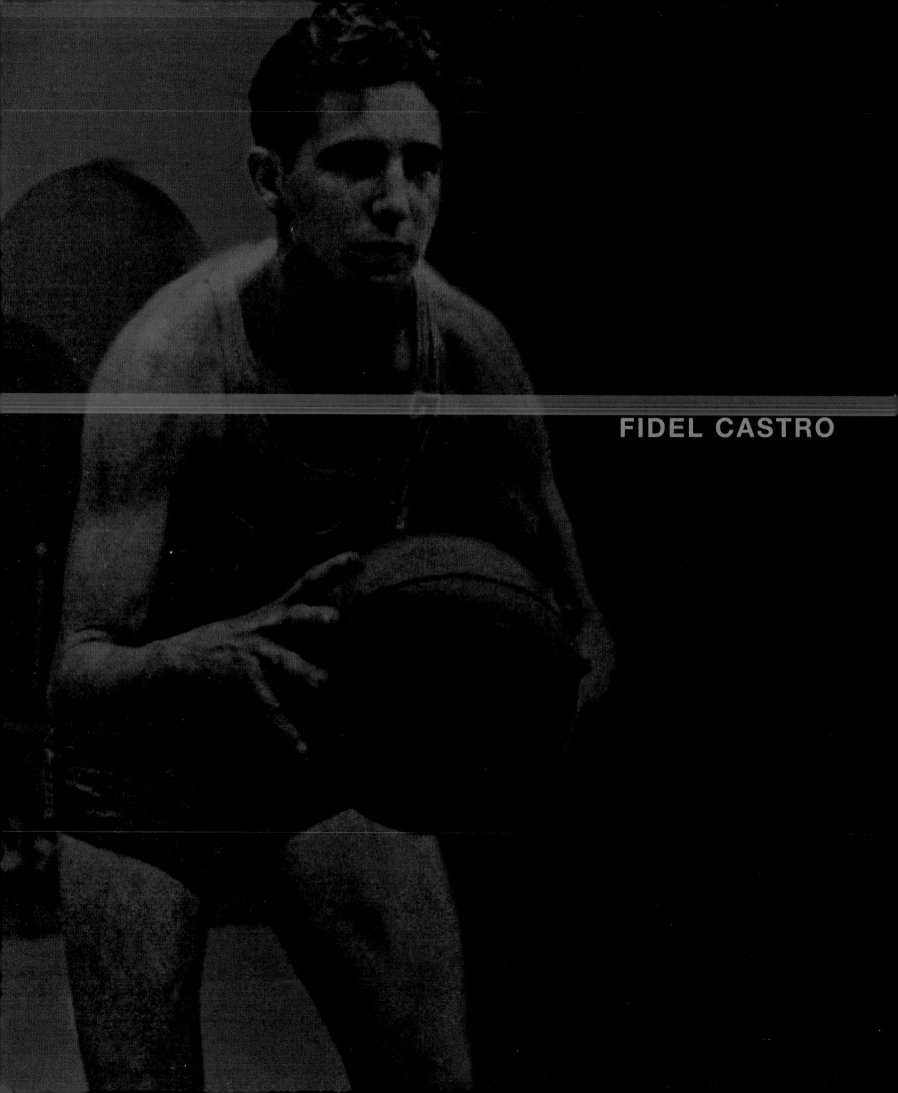

FIDEL CASTRO

HIS YOUTH

35 Fidel Castro, at the center of the photo in 1929, aged 3, between his sister Angelita, 6 years, and his brother Ramón, 4 years. The amount of care visible both in their persons and in their clothes demonstrates the well-off economic conditions of the family.

36 Fidel Castro, aged 17, photographed during a basketball training session – a sport in which he excelled while attending the Belén Jesuit College, Havana 1943.

HIS YOUTH

In his childhood, Fidel Castro grew within a contradiction which, for several years, characterized his beloved mother's existence. Lina Ruz González was a deeply Catholic woman who recited the rosary every night, but, at the same time found it impossible to fulfill her love for Angel Castro Argiz with the sacrament of marriage. He was already a married man and father of five.

Angel was Spanish and, at the end of the nineteenth century, had participated as a volunteer in the Spanish-American war. The war with which the decadent Spanish monarchy had tried in vain to conserve its last colony: Cuba. Repatriated, he returned to the island as an immigrant to try to find his luck. He found it thanks to his ability and his organizational capabilities. In 1905 he opened a small boarding house in Guaro which he called '*El Progresso*' and he started to organize groups of woodsmen for the cutting of wood which was needed as fuel for the sugar factories of the American United Fruit Company. In a short time he became wealthy, attained Cuban citizenship and married Maria Luisa Argota Reyes, daughter of one of the sugar factory's administrators.

Five children were born but the marriage failed because Maria Luisa couldn't bear life in the country anymore. She therefore left her husband and moved to Havana with her children. Angel, soon after, fell in love with Lina Ruz González the very young daughter of one of his collaborators, who loved him in return.

He was a strong and powerful 47-year-old man who always dressed elegantly. She was only 17 years old but in possession of a deep appeal: she used to ride miles and miles on horseback, through plantations, with a Colt in her belt to keep away brigands. She did not reject him, even though she had to wait for him to divorce his previous wife before she could become the new Mrs. Castro and give his surname to their children, whose number was ever-increasing. Angelita was born in 1923, Ramòn in 1925, Fidel on August 13th 1926, Raul in 1931, and the last one Emma was born in 1935.

Angel Castro was very wealthy: he owned 1800 hectares of sugar and fruit plant plantations in Biràn. He raised livestock (sheep, pigs, geese), kept on building houses which he subsequently rented, and he gave work to 600 laborers and farmers. Most of all he was loved by his employees. He treated them well, did not sack them during periods where work was scarce and he paid with his own money for their medical treatment.

At birth, Fidel weighed 12 lbs (5.5 kg). When he was 4 years old (his nickname was Titín) he asked and obtained permission to go to school with his older brothers and friends, thus learning to read and write at an early age. He ran barefoot in the fields and, every day after school, he would go to dive in the river with his brothers, the laborers' sons and his inseparable four dogs. He was an extremely good archer and – as he himself recalled in many interviews - often he would lead groups of boys who, equipped with sharp objects, would kill chickens, geese and even pigs in a sort of rodeo for the young. In such occasions his father was indulgent (those animals had been destined to be eaten anyway), but his mother Lina would belt the young and wild Fidel.

Castro was an excellent scholar. An avid reader of history books ever since he was a young boy, Castro was accepted in the La Salle Christian Brothers' school in Santiago only after he was baptized in the Cathedral on January 19th 1935 (a few days after his father's marriage to Lina). Six months afterwards he had his First Holy Communion. Castro had a strong disposition for sports and excelled in baseball and swimming, undertaking feats like diving in a dam where it was extremely dangerous and forbidden to dive. He also made pranks once in a while, like ringing doorbells. One day, Father Bernard punished him with a slap for every doorbell rung.

The time came for middle and secondary school, where he studied under the Jesuits in both times –first in Santiago and then in the renowned college of Belén in Havana. He would say of those years: "The Jesuits were very rigorous people. I learned, thanks to them, ethics and habits which were not just religious." The Jesuits reciprocated his high regard. In their final assessment they wrote: "He was always outstanding in every art and literature related field. A very good student and exceptional athlete, Fidel has earned everyone's admiration and affection. He possesses all the essential qualities and he will certainly be successful in life."

Then came his university phase where he attended the faculty of law. Here he met a group of communist students who induced him to read Marx. A new chapter started in his life.

FIDEL CASTRO El Líder Máximo: A Life in Pictures

40 Fidel Castro (left) with brothers
Raúl (center) and Ramón, wearing
the uniform of the Dolores de
Santiago de Cuba college which
was run by the Jesuits.

41 In the photograph on the right,
Fidel Castro, aged 10, pretends that
he is driving a tractor in his family
homestead at Biràn. His father was
the owner of sugarcane plantations
and farms covering a total of 4450
acres (1800 hectares).

42 In 1940 Santiago de Cuba, Fidel is here photographed in front of his step sister Lydia's residence. Lydia was born from his father's first marriage. It had been a year since he started studying at the La Salle Christian Brothers College.

43 A 13-year-old Fidel, (second from right) a pencil in his mouth, together with his classmates at the Dolores Santiago de Cuba College.

President of the United S-
tates.
If you like, give me a
ten dollars bill green american, in the letter, because
never, I have not seen a
ten dollars bill green american and I would like
to have one of them.
My address is:

    Sr. Fidel Castro
   Colegio de Dolores.
    Santiago de Cuba
     Oriente. Cuba.

I don't know very English
but I know very much
Spanish and I suppose
you don't know very Spa-
nish but you know very
English because you
are American but I am
not American.

(Thank you very much)
Good by. Your friend,

Fidel Castro

If you want iron to make
your sheaps ships I will
show to you the bigest
(minas) of iron of the land.
They are in Mayarí. Oriente
Cuba.

President of the United States.

If you like, give me a ten dollars bill green american, in the letter,

because never, I have not seen a ten dollar bill green

american and I would like to have one of them.

My address is:

Sr. Fidel Castro

Colegio de Dolores

Santiago de Cuba

Oriente. Cuba.

I don't know very English

but I know very much Spanish

and I suppose you don't know very Spanish but you know

very English because you are American but I am not American.

(Thank you very much.)

Good by. Your friend,

Fidel Castro

If you want iron to make your ships, I will show to you

the bigest (minas) of iron of the land.

They are in Mayarí, Oriente. Cuba.

44 On November 6th 1940, after having played a basketball game against a team of American students, the 14-year-old Castro decides to write a letter, in his broken English, to President Roosevelt where he asks him to send him 10 dollars. This request was not complied with.

47 A 17-year-old Fidel is here
photographed at Biràn while hunting
with one of his four dogs, with
which he loved to dive in the
dangerous and forbidden waters of
a dam. Besides being an excellent
marksman, the young Castro also
excelled in archery.

Fidel Castro que por su

48 In this commemorative photo taken in 1945, Fidel is awarded the honor of best athlete of Belén High School in Havana. He was confirmed as champion in volleyball, basketball, and most of all, baseball. He had become the star pitcher and had also earned the nickname "rey de la curva" (the king of the curve). In the high jump, he had also managed to jump a height of 5.75 ft (1.77 m)

49 After three years of university, Fidel has by now become the leader of the students' movement. The political culture of the student organizations in the University of Havana served as a launching point for some Cuban personalities, among whom Julio Antonio Mella and Fidel Castro.

FIDEL CASTRO

**FROM UNIVERSITY
TO THE TAKING
OF POWER**

52-53 An emblematic image: Castro is indicating an objective to his fellow militants; it's 1958 and Fidel is organizing the revolution on the Sierra Maestra.

54 Fidel Castro, photographed surrounded by children during a moment of relaxation in the vicinity of a sugar plantation in Havana. It's the summer of 1955 and he has just been released from prison following an amnesty. He had been imprisoned after the foiled attack on the Moncada Barracks. He is soon to leave for exile in Mexico and is wearing his customary beret and his military-style shirt.

FROM UNIVERSITY TO THE TAKING OF POWER

Young Fidel Castro first breathed the perfume of revolution in the classrooms of Havana University. There were many student assemblies and that impetuous young law school freshman immediately put his oratorical abilities to the test. He instilled enthusiasm in those hearing him and used to right tones and words to rally his audience. He was certainly a born speaker. The spirit of Christian solidarity with the poor, which he breathed in the long years spent with the Jesuits, had left its mark. Fidel wanted equality: he hated privilege, despised capitalists who – in his judgment – were only capable of exploiting the work of the humble. Soon he was to condemn private property in name of collectivization.

After the first street demonstrations in Cuba, he left for Bogotá. He went to protests against the assembly of the Organization of American States wanted by the U.S.A. And here he became a leader both for his organizational capacity and physical courage. After his law degree, which he obtained in 1950, Castro practiced law for short time, especially in the defense of political opponents of the regime, dissidents and young members of the clandestine communist movement, while personally joining the Orthodox Party and becoming one of its main spokesmen. But he was not one for democratic battles. He preferred armed conflicts. In 1952, Fulgencio Batista returned to the country, overthrew the government and instituted a strict dictatorship. For Castro it was time for an armed revolt, which culminated July 26th, 1953, with the assault on the Moncada Barracks. The attack backfired and was a massacre for his companions, while he and few other survivors were imprisoned on the Isle of Pines. After trial he was sentenced to 15 years of hard labor. Unexpectedly, in May 1955, Batista granted a general amnesty. Fidel went to Mexico in exile where he met "Che" Guevara and founded the "26th July Movement," in memory of the Moncada enterprise. His arrest and that of his comrades by the Mexican police followed in June 1956. After his release, two months later and upon the posting of a hefty bail, he and his comrades bought a yacht called *Granma*. He sailed with 82 armed comrades to disembark in Cuba. It was December 2nd, 1956. A second debacle awaited the insurgents: Batista's army was waiting for them. Out of the 82 comrades only Fidel and another 11 survived to spark off the guerilla warfare. Soon, though, the rebels became an army. Leading them was the foursome of Fidel, Raúl, "Che" Guevara and Camilo Cienfuegos.

The guerilla fighting lasted almost two full years. In fact, 1957 and 1958 were distinguished by ambushes, ferocious acts on both sides, fighters caught and burned alive, trains of Batista soldiers going to the front were derailed and the men killed by machine-gun fire. "Che" Guevara won the battle of Santa Clara, in the center of the island; Camilo Cienfuegos won the battle of Yaguajay. General Eulogio Cantillo, commander of the government troops, made a plea for negotiations. As soon as he heard the news, President Fulgencio Batista fled to Santo Domingo. On December 28th, 1958, "Radio Rebelde" ordered a general strike, while Guevara and Cienfuegos, leading their columns, headed for Havana. The order was to open fire on anyone offering resistance. In the meantime, Fidel, once occupied Santiago, nominated Manuel Urrutia, a magistrate friend of his, new President of the Republic, and decreed Santiago the temporary capital. Bloodshed followed. At the city's two military bases, Fort La Cabaña and the Columbia Barracks, they found undecided generals who no longer had any means of determining what they ought to do. Fidel reached Havana on January 8th.

A multitude of citizens was crowding the main roads. Castro entered Havana at 3.00 in the afternoon, standing on a tank. It was an apotheosis. He got into a jeep and reached the Presidential Palace where in the meantime Manuel Urrutia had moved in. From the terrace of the building he addressed a crowd of over 100,000 delirious people. His speech began with these words: "I think that if we managed to put an army together by starting with just twelve people who left no wounded behind, nor ever shot a prisoner, we deserve the command of the forces of the Republic." An ovation followed. While Castro spoke, a dove from a nearby park came and sat on his shoulder. He freed it into the air with a gesture which none of the tens of thousands present will ever be able to forget.

FIDEL CASTRO El Líder Máximo: A Life in Pictures

58 and 59 This public demonstration was organized in Havana 1950 by the "Orthodox Party" which fought against Batista. Top, leading the procession, Castro (circled) is the second from right. In the big photograph on the right, Fidel is raised in triumph by his supporters during another demonstration against the regime.

60 and 61 Between August and December 1953, the few rebels, Castro and his brother Raul among them, who had escaped the massacre which followed the failed attack on the Moncada Barracks, were arrested and subjected to harsh sentences. Left, Fidel is taken to the interrogation room where (top) he responds contemptuously to the questions directed to him. Right, Fidel Castro's mug shot.

FIDEL CASTRO

62 and 63 Havana 1952: Fidel Castro, a young lawyer, is pictured here in the law office where he worked for some time dedicating himself to the defense of political prisoners. It was during that period that he gave life to the first clandestine army formation intended for the assault on the Moncada Barracks of July 26th 1953.

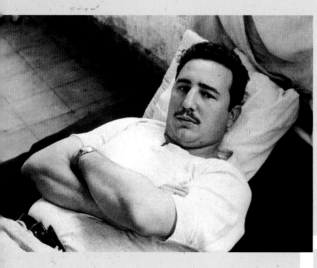

1956

64 and 65 Left, the future leader of the Cuban revolution is photographed here in July 12th 1956 at Mexico City in prison after being arrested by the police with the charge of having led a riot. Sometime later, Castro and his comrades where released after the posting of a hefty bail. Right, having just been released from prison, Fidel is photographed in a modest apartment in which he had found refuge in.

66 and 67 Bottom, Fidel Castro and "Che" Guevara are pictured in their Mexican cell in July 1956. Guevara is bare-chested and clean-shaven. It is the first photo which pictures them together. Right, Fidel and his comrades leave prison.

68 and 69 These three pictures show Fidel
Castro, in the Sierra Maestra, while giving
instructions to his guerillas, the number of
which keeps increasing despite checkpoints
and raids made by Fulgencio Batista's men.

FIDEL CASTRO

70 and 71 Top, Autumn, 1957, Fidel Castro is surrounded by his men in the Sierra Maestra. Right, a close-up of Fidel, his inseparable rifle and telescope in hand, standing in-front of his "commando" which has settled itself in a hay-covered hut.

72 Fidel Castro (standing, bowed)
and "Che" Guevara (first on the left,
crouched) as they plan an attack
with their men.

73 Fidel's (sitting on the left)
comrades, which have started to let
their beards grow, listen to the news
being read from the newspaper.

1957

74 and 75 These two photos show Fidel Castro and "Che" Guevara in the Sierra Maestra. It was here that their strong friendship fortified. When they met, in Mexico, where both had been taking refuge after their failed revolt attempts, in Cuba and Argentina respectively, Ernesto Guevara had told Fidel and his comrades; "I will remain always with you. Call me "Che." In his dialect, that word meant "mine."

1958

FIDEL CASTRO

76-77 Fidel Castro, sitting on a hammock, reads an illustrated magazine. The glasses he is wearing show that, still young, he suffered from presbyopia.

78 and 79 In the photo on the left, Fidel is pictured as he writes a letter containing military instructions to one of his task force's units in the Sierra Maestra,1958. Right, he is talking to a group of guerilla, among which the first one on the left is his companion Celia Sánchez and, next to her, Vilma Espin, another revolutionary, attentively listens to him.

80 and 81 Top, Fidel inspects a
group of his fighters who have, by
now, reached about 800 men. Right,
Castro, with his brother Raúl (in-
front of him, wearing glasses) and
his comrades, is intent on picking
up enemy radio transmissions.

82-83 The commander, cigar in mouth, is surrounded by his fighters and supporters, many of which very young. By now we are close to the defeat of Fulgencio Batista's army and the seizure of the Havana.

1958

84-85 In an encampment in the
Sierra Maestra, Fidel Castro,
with his companion Celia Sánchez
on his left, smiles and listens
to a guitar performance.

86 and 87 The photo on top was taken on September 3rd 1958. Fidel, microphone in hand, is making a speech to his comrades who are recording it on tape so that those who could not attend would be able to listen to it. Right, A military image of "El Líder máximo" in war attire and holding his inseparable rifle.

1958

1959

88-89 This picture goes back to the end of December 1958. Fidel Castro, leading his rebels, starts to the march for the freedom of Havana. Only a few days remain until the seizure of power.

90-91   Fidel talks with the crowd which expresses appreciation and trust towards him. On January 5th , Manuel Urrutia, nominated by Fidel as Head of State, arrived to Havana together with his ministers, and had established himself in the Columbia barrack.

92 and 93 Soon after his entrance in the city, leading an army of 8500 partisans, Castro offers himself to the crowd in a Havana street. Seeing the eagerness with which a young girl salutes him, he stops the jeep, affectionately raises the child in his arms and shows her to the crowd.

1959

94 Fidel gazes at the crowd which applauds him: the intense expression on his face betrays the tension of the moment.

96 and 97 Left, Castro shows to the crowd the portrait a fan makes for him. The words read "Fidel el libertador" (Fidel the liberator). Right, a moment of the famous speech made on the terrace of the presidential palace in the afternoon of January 8th 1959.

1959

98 and 99 Fidel Castro has left the
tank with which he entered Havana
and has climbed on the jeep which
will take him to the presidential
palace. From there he will address
the crowd and narrate them all
details of the great battles won by
"Che" Guevara at Santa Clara and
by Camilo Cienfuegos at Yaguajay.

100-101 Hundreds of hands rise towards "El Líder Maximo", author of a rapid and bloodless revolution.

102-103 Fidel Castro offers himself to the Cubans in the convulsive hours of the taking of power. In effect, the occupation of the principal cities and of Havana was a triumphant march across the country, with Batista's guards defeated.

104 and 105 Right, Fidel autographs a poster. Left, Castro salutes the crowd. Shortly before, he had climbed down from his jeep to embrace his young, 10-year old son, Fidelito. Castro had recognized, amongst the crowd, the boy whose hand was being held by Lydia, Castro's step sister.

106 and 107 Left, a bus transports a group of "barbudos" (bearded ones) towards the capital. Top, Fidel is crossing the capital on a tank captured from the regular troops.

108-109 It's January 8th 1959. Batista has fled: the crowd cheers at the fall of the regime.

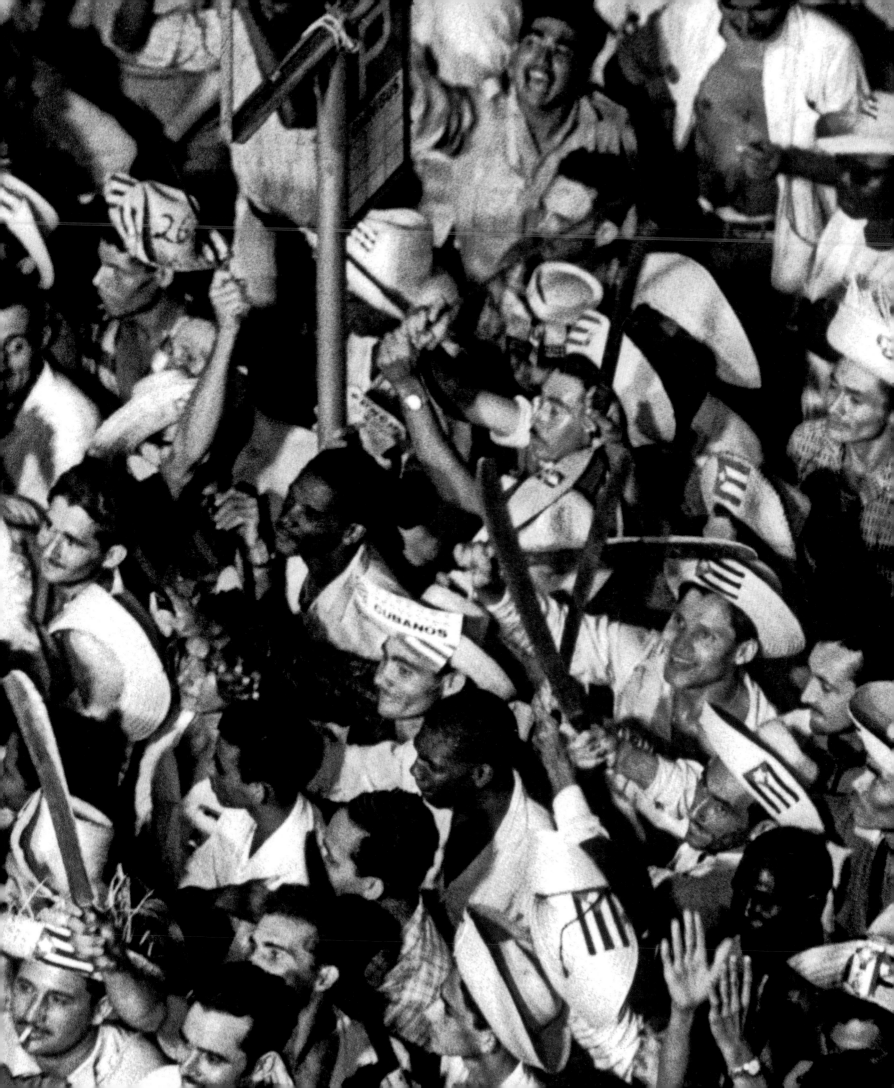

110-111 Left, on January 8th, 1959 a huge crowd listens to Fidel as he addresses them from the presidential palace terrace. Right, a close-up of the "Líder" during his speech which lasted almost four hours. Among other things, Castro promised the citizens freedom from exploitation and announced harsh punishments for those responsible for the Batista repression.

111

112 and 113 Fidel, surrounded by
his bodyguards, passes through
Havana streets at the end of the
exalting day of January 8th 1959,
and continues to salute the delirious
crowd.

1959

114-115 This famous
photo immortalizes an episode which
greatly benefited the revolution's
iconography: a dove flew and sat on
Fidel Castro's shoulders as he
pronounces his victory speech on the
afternoon of January 8th, 1959. The
commander took the dove in his
hands and freed it in the air with a
gesture with which he wanted to give
a clear symbolic meaning.

116-117 Castro reads those newspapers which report news of his triumphant entrance in Havana. Fidel held in high regard the judgment of the foreign press and had very good personal relationships with correspondents of the most popular newspapers, even American ones.

118 and 119 Left, Fidel Castro talks
with the new Head of State he
himself nominated, Manuel Urrutia,
whose name appears, together with
that of the "Líder" in the posters
held up by the crowd (right).

1959

120-121 Fidel Castro and Urrutia, the magistrate he chose to lead the revolutionary government, sign the first administrative measures. Following the victory celebrations, everyone is now wearing civilian attire, except Fidel Castro who will keep on wearing his uniform.

FIDEL CASTRO

El Líder Máximo: A Life in Pictures   El Líder Máximo: A Life in Pictures   El Líder Máximo: A Life in Pictures

**AFTER THE
REVOLUTION
THE FIRST 40 YEARS**

125 Fidel Castro, during his first trip
to the United States in April 1959,
looks up at Abraham Lincoln's
statue in Washington after having
laid a wreath at its feet.

126 During his first visit to the
United States, the new Cuban
leader shakes hands with Richard
Nixon, the American vice president.
Hostility toward the U.S is still
far away.

AFTER THE REVOLUTION THE FIRST 40 YEARS

The measures which Castro imposed on his country immediately after taking power were exactly those he preached and had promised at the time of the revolution: the confiscation of foreign property and all Cuban owned land of more than 990 acres (400 hectares); the reduction of rent by 50 percent to favor tenants rather than owners; the nationalization of companies; the abolition of trade unions and freedom of the press; the expropriation of casinos, which were to be successively managed by the State and only accessible to foreign tourists. In the meantime "Che" Guevara was in charge of getting rid of the Batista regime collaborationists. Under his power, the revolutionary tribunals installed themselves in Fort La Cabaña and "Operation Truth" began: 150 death sentences and many suicides in prison resulted. The international press called it a bloodbath. The total embargo that the U.S. decreed against Cuba and the absolute ban of American tourists visiting the island brought about the immediate collapse of the Cuban economy. The hitherto ruling class began escaping abroad (especially to America), but so did many disappointed with the revolution. The sugar production crumbled, given the managerial inexperience of the public administrators. During this period the U.S.S.R. intervened in support, financing Castro's regime. This was in exchange for authorization to install missile ramps; this event nearly led to a third world war. In a few years, Soviet aid made up a quarter of Cuba's gross domestic product. In exchange, the Cubans organized the summit of communist countries in 1966, thus contributing to dividing the world between pro-U.S.A and pro-U.S.S.R. nations. At the time, the U.S.A. was already heavily committed in Vietnam). In Cuba's internal politics and programs, literacy, health and tourism represented positive initiatives. In the speech which he gave in fall 1960 to the UN (his first speech before the New York-based assembly), Castro solemnly announced that "Cuba will soon be the first nation in the Americas without a single illiterate person."

He had immediately initiated a far-reaching education program, mobilizing 270,000 teachers and university students in literacy programs for laborers and *campesinos*. In just one year, the illiteracy rate was reduced by 20 percent. The "National Cuban Museum" was born; it still holds 700,000 letters of gratitude sent to Castro by ex-illiterates.

Progress was also made in economics, in particular in the production of sugar, which in 1969-70 reached nearly 10 million tons. In the meantime, with the first U.S.A.-U.S.S.R. peacemaking steps, Washington in 1975 revoked the sanctions against Cuba. They were to be re-enacted, though upon the outbreak of internal conflicts and civil wars in Nicaragua, Guatemala and El Salvador. In 1979 the "Movement of Non-Aligned Nations" was born, and Castro became its president. According to NATO, though, they were "aligned" with the U.S.S.R. At the first world congress, in Havana, Marshal Tito was among the welcome guests. There were 94 delegations from different countries and UN Secretary-General Kurt Waldheim also came in from New York. Castro began with a surprising speech "The Yankee imperialists and their allies old and new (with particular reference to the Chinese government) did not want this meeting to take place in Cuba. They therefore constructed the lie that Cuba wanted to change the movement into an instrument of Soviet politics. False!" There were underlying clashes between China and U.S.S.R. for hegemony in the East (conflicts in Indochina, Cambodia against Vietnam, Pakistan against Afghanistan) and hostile policies toward Israel, considered a U.S. satellite in the Middle East. Unconditional support was given to the Ayatollah Khomeini'a Islamic Revolution in Iran. In those years, Castro had an important role as a mediator in conflicts with Islamic factions (the Iran-Iraq war and the Turkish-Greek conflict in Cyprus). He was to give his support, though, to the Soviet invasion of Afghanistan in 1979. In 1989, with the fall of the Berlin wall, the implosion of real communism, Castro was to remain faithful to his political creed. He conserved good economic and diplomatic relations with Moscow, but avoided following its ideological route. Eloquent, to this regard, was a famous phrase he pronounced in 1995: "The fall of socialism in some countries does not mean it has failed: it has lost a battle." In the early 1990s, however, the first breaks came in the anti-American policy of the Cuban leader. The tough and inexorable hostility of the White House and the American embargo of goods and people to Cuba could not be borne forever. The export-import ban against the island had lasted for nearly 40 years. Perhaps it was in search for a mediation that in 1996 Castro visited the Vatican, where Pope John Paul II received him cordially. In January 1998, the pope returned the visit, openly exhorting Washington to lift the embargo. A gesture of great generosity and call for peace: an inevitable boost to the image of the dictator, nearing old age.

FIDEL CASTRO

El Líde

El Líder Máximo: A Life in Pictures

FIDEL CASTRO

130 and 131 Fidel Castro talks to the members of the American Society of Newspaper Editors in Washington. Open contention with the U.S will explode on October 12th 1961, with the start of the "Caribbean Crisis," which was caused by the discovery of the Soviet missiles that had been installed in Cuba.

132 and 133 Left, during a party at the Overseas Press Club in Washington, Castro shows with amusement a newspaper dated 17th March which has, as its headline, the news of a plot to kill him. Five killers had arrived to Cuba from Philadelphia. To the journalists asking him for a comment, Castro replied: "I sleep well and I don't worry about anything." Right, Fidel salutes the journalists at the end of the party.

134 and 135 Top, accompanied by high-level U.S. Army officials during his first trip to America since his taking of power, Castro visits the Bronx zoo and is pictured here eating an ice cream cone. In the photo on the right, four pretty members of the Photo Reporters Club of New York hand him a certificate.

136 and 137 Top, Fidel Castro discusses with some Cuban landowners the significance and importance of the new agrarian reform law which he signed (photo on the right) sometime after the expulsion of Batista. Among other things the reform forbade the ownership of property larger than 990 acres (400 hectares).

1959

138 Fidel at work as president of the
National Land Reform Institute. Left,
Antonio Nuñez Jimenez, Director of
the Institute and (right) the economist
Oscar Pino Santos, both implementers
of the first collectivist law launched by
the new government.

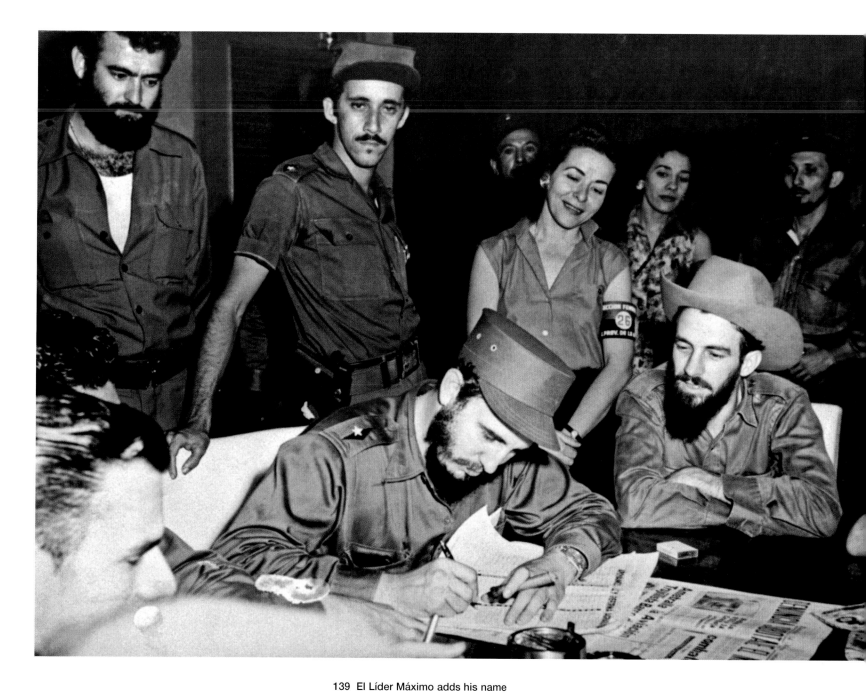

139 El Líder Máximo adds his name
to the million signatures gathered by
the "26th July" Movement as a
support to the agrarian reform
which was harshly contested by the
big landowners, most of them
foreign (American), but supported
by the "campesinos."

140-141 Castro, whom we see here during a meeting with a group of students in Havana, always considered his rapport with students as important, particularly with grade school students. In the first years of the revolution the country's basic literacy program was carried on intensely.

1959

1960

142 and 143 Castro as he inaugurates the "A. Echeverria" Citta Universitaria, (University City) Havana in the autumn of 1960. As from the start, the development of education, the diffusion of culture together with the development of sanitation, and tourism, embodied one of the key points of Castro's programs.

144-145 Fidel Castro opens the games with a kick-off during the opening ceremony held for the Central American Countries' soccer championship, which started in Cuba in February 1960. Soccer always has been one of the Cuban leader's favorite sports.

146 and 147 Besides soccer, Castro

had also been a keen baseball player

in his youth. Left, we see him

IDEL CASTRO El Líder Máximo: A Life in Pictures

1960

150-151 Fidel gets ready to leave on a speedboat for a fishing spree on Treasure Lake. On his right, special guest Anastas Mikoyan, the Soviet vice president who came to Cuba to offer cheaply priced petroleum, weapons and advantageous loans to the new government.

1960

152 Fidel Castro and Ernest Hemingway, the American writer who had settled in Cuba, had in common their love for fishing. Left, during the annual fishing tournament, held in Hemingway's honor on May 13th 1960, Castro catches a marlin fish weighing 54 lbs (24.5 kg).

153 Castro, standing next to Hemingway, holds the three silver trophies awarded during the depth fishing contest, which ended on May 15th 1960.

154-155 The Líder Máximo in discussion with the writer, who had decided to settle in Cuba.

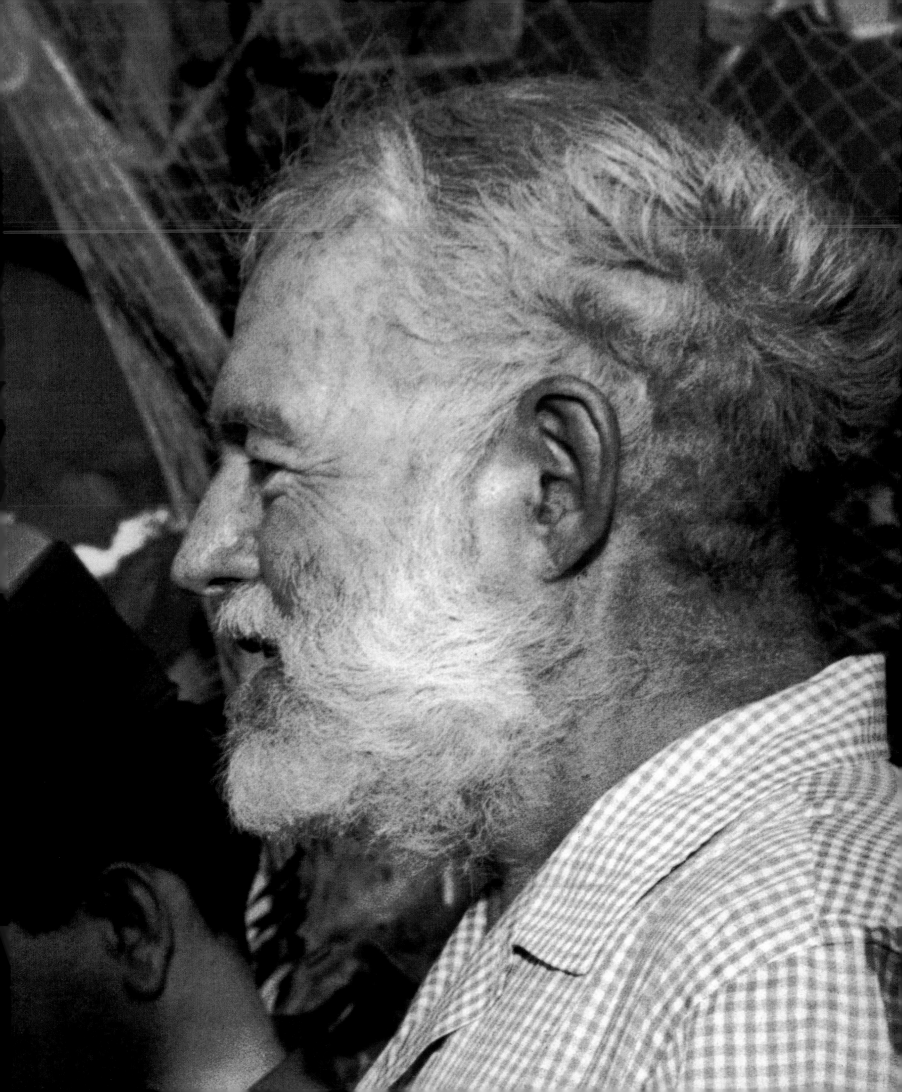

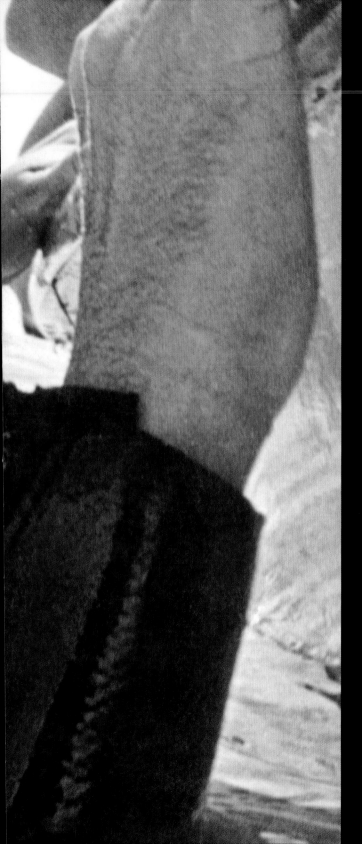

1960

156-157 The sea, swimming and fishing once again: Fidel has just concluded a scuba dive; he is wearing a wetsuit and has pulled off his diving mask. Passion for aquatic sport activities will always remain one of his characteristics.

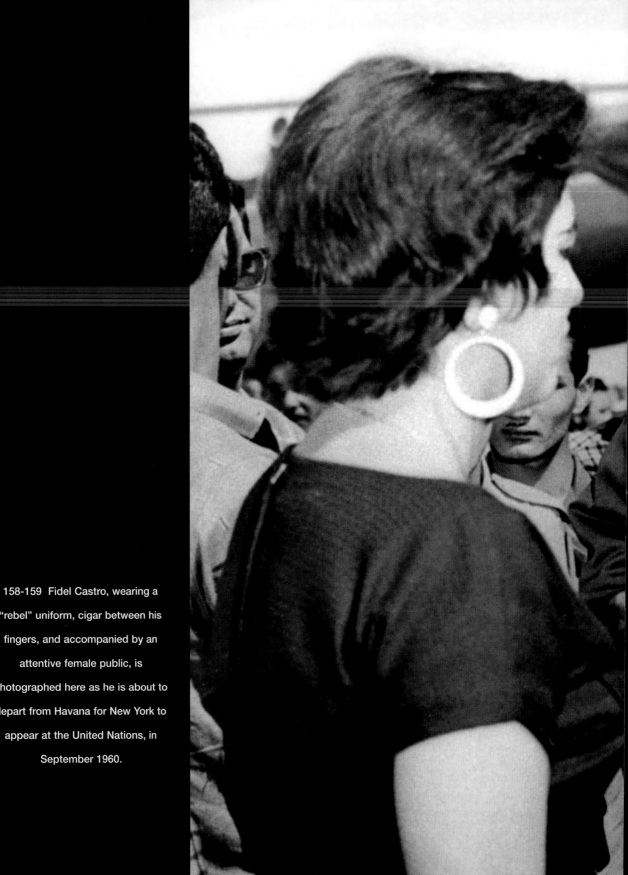

158-159 Fidel Castro, wearing a "rebel" uniform, cigar between his fingers, and accompanied by an attentive female public, is photographed here as he is about to depart from Havana for New York to appear at the United Nations, in September 1960.

1960

160 and 161 Fidel has nominated
his brother Raúl (photo on the left,
in the car with him on the front seat)
as his foreign affairs minister. Raúl
will accompany Fidel to New York
during his visit to the United Nations
where he will be welcomed by a
small crowd of fans (photo at top.)

162 and 163 Top, Castro is surrounded by journalists upon his arrival to New York for his United Nations appearance in September 14th 1960. Since he was not satisfied with the hotel that had been reserved for him, he moved to the Harlem's Hotel Theresa, in the heart of the "black" district, where he and his entourage, occupied 40 rooms. Right, Castro attentively reads an account of his visit to the U.S as reported by a Spanish-language newspaper.

1960

164 and 165 Three photos of the cordial meeting between Fidel Castro and the Soviet leader Nikita Khrushchev, during their stay in New York for the United Nations' conference. It was during this occasion that Fidel's anti-American inclination became apparent.

166 and 167 Since the very beginnings of his taking of power in Cuba, Fidel Castro showed the world where his sympathies lay: toward the third world countries. Top, during a discussion with the Indian leader Nehru. Right, smiling as he stands next to the Egyptian president Gamal Abder Nasser.

168 and 169 Two of Fidel Castro's expressions during his speech to the United Nations in September 14th 1960. Following the challenge openly thrown by him against Washington, the U.S prohibits the entry of people and merchandise in to Cuba.

170 Ten years from the revolution,
despite economic difficulties, Fidel
has established a now consolidated
regime in Isla Grande. In Castro's
eyes lay all the hopes for Cuba's
future and, between his fingers, his
ever-present Cohiba cigars.

1970

172 and 173 Increases in sugarcane cultivation is one of the tenets of the new regime. Fidel Castro does not limit himself to just issuing decrees, but provides an example by wearing farming gear and working in the fields. Here we see him at the start of the 70's, busy in person, in cutting cane, production of which, at the time, totaled about 10 million tons a year.

1970

174 and 175 After the cutting of the sugar cane, Fidel talks with the farmers and their sons about the harvest. He is wearing a white t-shirt, work trousers, a wide brimmed straw hat, with the ever-present cigar in hand.

1971

176 and 177 Top, Fidel arrives in Santiago del Chile on November 10th 1971 and is welcomed by President Salvador Allende (on his left). Right, he is here shaking hands with the miners of the "El Teniente" mining camp which had been owned by the Americans and had been recently nationalized.

178 and 179 We are in Chile, in November 1971. After having visited the "El Teniente" mine at Sewell (left), Fidel is teaching basketball to the workers and their children (right). This display has a precise socio-political significance: work and leisure for the working class.

180 and 181 Fidel is talking in Revolution Square, Havana, under the gigantic marble statue of José Martí. During his speeches the leader continually gesticulates with his index finger in his typical oratorical manner.

182-183 In this photo, taken during Castro's trip to Algeria in May 1972, President Boumedienne (half-hidden behind the officer in the foreground) helps Castro get down from a camel.

184 Castro, during an official visit in
Vietnam in October 1973, is greeted
by the Prime Minister Pham Van
Dong in the Hanoi airport. It is a visit
of a clear political anti-American
significance.

185 Still in Hanoi, Castro waves the
North Vietnamese flag and is
celebrated by Vietnamese women
who have fought against the
Americans, and now wear
campaigns medals on their tunics.

186 and 187 Fidel, in the first photo,

deep in thought and surrounded by

the customary smoke cloud, (left)

next photographed during voting in

the Cuban Parliamentary election in

August 4th 1979.

FIDEL CASTRO

1977

189 This photo immortalizes Castro, on April 4th 1977, during his visit to the U.S.S.R, which is considered to be Cuba's leading supporter. The Cuban President is greeted in Moscow's airport by Leonid Brezhnev, the First Secretary of the Soviet Communist Party.

190 and 191 Caught during two
relaxing moments, Fidel seems to
be reflecting on the consequences
of the American embargo and of his
pro-Russian inclinations, in years
(we are in the 70's) when the world
is divided in two factions.

192-193 In 1979 Castro is
nominated President of the
Movement of Non-Aligned Nations,
a title he will hold until 1983.

FIDEL CASTRO

1979

1981

194 Fidel visits the U.S.S.R in February 1981 to celebrate the twenty years of the Russian-Cuban friendship and talks beneath Lenin's picture at the Odessa Opera House (Ukraine).

1983

196-197 March 1983: Fidel Castro
and the Palestinian leader Yasser
Arafat shake hands and give the
victory sign during the seventh
summit of the Non-Aligned Nations
in New Delhi, India.

1984

198 and 199 June 28th 1984, Castro, with his ever-present cigar, together with Jesse Jackson (left), the Afro-American candidate for the presidential nomination, to whom he has just delivered a group of 48 Cuban and American political prisoners. This is the first sign of an opening to the U.S. Top, Jackson and the freed prisoners leave for Washington from the José Martí airport in Havana.

1984

FIDEL CASTRO El Líder Máximo: A Life in Pictures

200 and 201 Two intense close-ups
of El Líder Máximo at the beginning
of the 80's: The hair is graying, the
cigar remains indispensable.

1986

203 Havana, February 8th 1986:

Fidel Castro talks to the delegates

of the third congress of the Cuban

Communist Party beneath the

photos of the three "martyrs of the

revolution." Mella, Cienfuegos, and

"Che" Guevara.

FIDEL CASTRO

204 Mikhail Gorbachov (close-up) has just arrived in the airport of Havana and is welcomed by a formal and restrained Fidel Castro. It's April 2nd 1989 and there is less warmth towards the new Russian leader compared with that shown towards his predecessors. The fall of the Berlin wall is near.

206 An intense close-up of Fidel Castro's face where signs of his aging are starting to show. It's February 29th 1993 and the first democratic election since 1959 has just been concluded. Castro has been re-confirmed president with the overwhelming majority of votes.

208-209 Havana celebrates Fidel's 68th birthday on August 13th 1994. Near Castro's poster there is one of an officer killed in attempting to thwart the escape of a group of Cubans to Florida.

1993

1997

El Líder Máximo: A Life in Pictures El Líder Máximo: A Life in Pictures

211 On October 17th 1997 in Havana, funeral rites for Guevara and six of his fighters took place. Their remains had been returned to Cuba by the Bolivian government. Castro gave the funeral oration on that occasion, standing beneath a bas-relief which captures Guevara's intense expression.

1997

212 and 213 Left, on the occasion of
the start of the 1997-1998 scholastic
year, Castro talks to children and
teachers beneath a large poster of
"Che" Guevara. Right, Castro feels
moved after receiving a white rose
during the "Pedagogy 1997"
convention in Havana.

214-215 Castro meets the South
African president, Nelson Mandela at
Geneva's WTO on May 19th 1998.

216 and 217 On January 21st 1998, Havana witnessed a historic event: the first Papal visit. John Paul II stayed five days in Cuba and was gratified by the enthusiasm show by the entire population.

1998

218 and 219 Fidel was full of care
and attention during Pope John
Paul visit to Cuba, which started on
January 21st and ended on the
25th. On his speech made in
Revolution Square, the Pope hoped
for "the birth of a society able to
offer peace, justice and freedom"
and warned about the harm of
excessive capitalism.

220 and 221 During 1996 Fidel Castro visited various nations in a more receptive tone compared with that of the preceding decades. Top, he is photographed during his official visit to Paris. Right, a moment of meditation during the Ibero-American summit taking place at the Viña del Mar, in Chile.

FIDEL CASTRO

El Líder Máximo: A Life in Pictures El Líder Máximo: A Life in Pictures El Líder Máximo: A Life in Pictures

**AND EL LÌDER
DOMINATED FOR
HALF A CENTURY**

224 The start of the third millennium coincided for Cuba with a period of economic crisis caused by Russia's dwindling help. Castro reacts with energy by developing scientific resources and turning the island into a world center of biotechnologies.

226 Aged in body but not in spirit, Castro looks for new allies without denying the country's autarky which he kept on with vigor despite the American embargo.

AND EL LÌDER DOMINATED FOR HALF A CENTURY

In the long and fascinating story of Fidel Castro there were not a few episodes of violence and terrorism, guilt resting on both sides of the conflict. The United States started, with the CIA trying to poison "El Líder." A renowned American journalist, George Crile, discovered this and published the facts. The attempt took place with the help of some mafia bosses, including Santo Trafficante, a casino owner who lost his assets after Castro nationalized them. Then came the bomb on the Cuban plane which in 1976 caused 73 victims, and in 1983 the invasion of Grenada ordered by Reagan ended with a bloodbath. Eleven years later Castro's Coast Guard criminally sank the *13 de Marzo* which was trying to make the crossing to Florida: 41 refugees were killed.

Between the end of 1979 and the beginning of 1980 the "Embassy crisis" took place in Havana: thousands of citizens took to the embassies seeking political asylum. After much give and take, some 150,000 dissidents were granted authorization to leave for the United States from the port of Mariel. They went down in history as the "marielitos."

In the context of the United Nations, Castro ended up becoming the spokesman for underdeveloped nations (and a real legend). They formed the "Group of 77" and they elected him as their leader. After having formulated tough criticisms of the current international economic order, Castro convoked an assembly of world economists. In the course of this they were forced to accept that they could no longer ignore multinationals in dealing with the development of the world economy, insofar as the multinationals owned the technology, the markets and the financial resources. During that summit, the multinational interests had to bitterly admit that "The policy of using force has no future."

With the beginning of the third millennium, instead, the attitude toward freedom of the press changed. Castro became more comprehensive, accepted criticism, even on occasion inviting it. To journalists, the leader suggested adopting "a critical spirit which should not destroy nor castigate. You must fight against censure and self-censure without forgetting your role as educators, though. Please be less bored, less timorous and give less room to apologetic language."

Aid and solidarity from the U.S.S.R. dwindled after 1985 (with the advent of Gorbachov). But starting from 1990, after the collapse of communism in Russia and Eastern Europe, Cuba had to fatally restrain its geopolitical ambitions. Its diplomatic prestige had gone, exports to sugar at advantageous conditions to the U.S.S.R. had ended and the product lost value. A severe economic crisis ensued and the government was forced to adopt austerity measures. Starting from the mid-1990s, Castro's government sought a new solution in developing biotechnology. Cuba thus became on of the most important exporters of medical technology and pharmaceutical patents.

Regarding the conflicting rapport with the United States, the tragic attack of September 11, 2001 on the Twin Towers disgusted Castro, who manifested the utmost solidarity with Bush. This was a beginning of peaceful times between Havana and Washington, which finally authorized the export of food products to the island.

As of 2004, the economy and living conditions in Cuba began to improve. At this point in his parable, when he could finally rest a little on his island, in mid summer 2006, disease attacked Fidel.

Was Fidel Castro a victim of a personality cult? Even though it was difficult to avoid, facilitated by the mass media of the whole world, one cannot say that he wanted it and promoted it. He proved available to respond to all interview requests which came to him from famous as well as unknown journalists, allowing armies of photographers and cameramen to portray him. By his own decision he was portrayed on only two stamps: on one issued in 1974 on the occasion of the visit of Leonid Brezhnev, and on the one issued "in commemoration of the 40th anniversary of the seizure of power." Much more venerated and mythicized were the two great fallen of the "revolución," "Che" Guevara and Camilo Cienfuegos.

: A Life in Pictures

231 Fidel stands at attention in
front of the flag held by boxing
champion Félix Savón during the
ceremonial salute for the Cuban
athletes team which is leaving for
the Olympic Games held in Sydney
in September 2000.

232 and 233 The U.S.S.R has ceased to exist, but Cuba's relations with Eastern Europe continue in a climate of cordiality. (Left) Castro receives a tribute from two young members of a Ukraine delegation in June 2000; Bottom, he greets the Russian president Vladmir Putin who visits Havana in December 2000.

2000

2001

234 Fidel Castro goes for his first
state visit to Iran on May 8th 2001;
In the photo he is next to the
President Mohammad Khatami
inside the monumental complex of
Saad-Abad in Teheran.

235 Cuba's friendly relationship with Arabic countries remains as intense as ever. Castro, upon his arrival to the Doha airport, is welcomed by the Emir of Qatar, Sheikh Hamad bin Khalifa Al Thani on May 13th 2001.

236-237 Fidel Castro prepares to talk during the World Conference against Racism on September 1st 2001 in Durban, South Africa. The Líder Máximo's health is starting to decline but Fidel gives no hint of stopping.

2OO2

238 and 239 Top, Fidel participates
in an auction during the "Cigar
Festival" taking place in Havana in
March 2002. Right, engaged in a
game of chess against his young
nephew Lázaro Castro during the
international championship which
takes place every year in Havana.

240 and 241 The mixture of
nationalism and populism which
characterizes the regime appears
evident in these two pictures: a
demonstration of solidarity in favor
of the Venezuelan president Hugo
Chavez (left) and the celebration of
the 1st May in Cuba (right).

2002

242-243 A peculiar expression of Fidel Castro next to the American ex-president Jimmy Carter during the latter's visit to Havana in May 2002. Carter was the first important American politician to visit Cuba after Castro's seizure of power in 1959. This was a sign of cordiality which followed Fidel's harsh condemnation of the terrorist attack on the Twin Towers of September 11th 2001.

2002

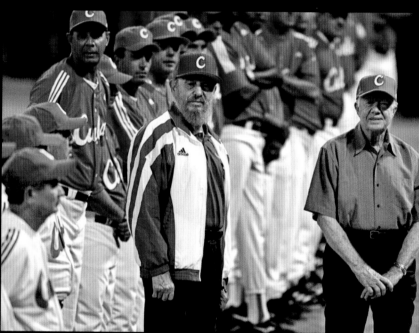

2002

244 and 245 During Jimmy Carter's
visit to Cuba, Castro in the presence
of the American ex-president (top),
inaugurates the baseball
championship with the first throw of
the ball (left).

246 and 247 Castro participates in the celebrations taking place at Cárdenas for the 10th birthday of Elián Gonzáles, the boy at the center of a dispute between his Cuban father and his mother's relatives who had escaped to Dallas. The case had been resolved with the return of the boy, an important success for the Cuban diplomacy.

248 and 249 Two more pictures from Elián Gonzáles' birthday: (left) Castro talking with one of Elián's schoolmates (top) Watching while the boy blows out his birthday candle.

250-251 Fidel laughs to minimize the error – almost a diplomatic gaffe – which he had just made during his speech in Asunción: he said "Uruguay" instead of "Paraguay".

2003

252-253 Castro photographed while taking photos in Asunción as he waits for President Duarte to give start to the opening ceremony for the Paraguay's Social Entities meeting.

254 and 255 The sequence of Castro's grievous fall (soon becoming famous all over the world) which occurred on Friday October 20th 2004, during a ceremony for the ordination of the scholastic diplomas in Santa Clara. Castro tripped on a step as he descended the platform and fell down on his right side, hitting first his knee, his ankle and then his elbow and arm. Some minutes later he himself reassured the 11 million spectators who were watching the event live.

2004

FIDEL CASTRO — El Líder Máximo: A Life in Pictures

256 and 257 Havana, Saturday December 2nd 2006: it's the 50th anniversary of the day in which Castro and his "rebels" began the revolution. Fidel has not made a public appearance since the end of July, that is, since he transferred full power to his brother Raúl. The latter does not disclose the reasons for Fidel's failure to participate in the celebration, thus allowing for the worst conjectures.

On the occasion, Raúl Castro holds a meeting in Revolution Square where he recalls the harsh conflict against the United Sates which, in a way, is still going on with the persistence of a partial embargo against the island. Feeling moved, he recalls the demonstrations made in favor of Cuba, like the one which occurred in Mexico City, during May two years previously (photo on the right)

258 and 259 Fidel, of Catholic upbringing, shows a particular openness also towards other religions, in particular towards Orthodox Christian. Top, he accompanies the Patriarch Bartholomew I who is on an official visit to Havana in January 2004. Right, while waiting for the inauguration of the Greek Orthodox Cathedral in Havana Castro spends some time talking with the nuns of Saint Bridget.

2005

260-261 A large crowd welcomes the Venezuelan president Hugo Chavez during his visit to Cuba on Saturday 21st April 2005. Chavez had always been a supporter of Castro's ideas and was very close to him during his months of illness, appearing with him on TV on January 15th 2007 and interviewing him on radio on February 28th.

From 262 to 269 In the summer of 2006, Castro makes public appearances in the months preceding his hospital admission. His face appears strained but his strong fiber keeps on sustaining him.

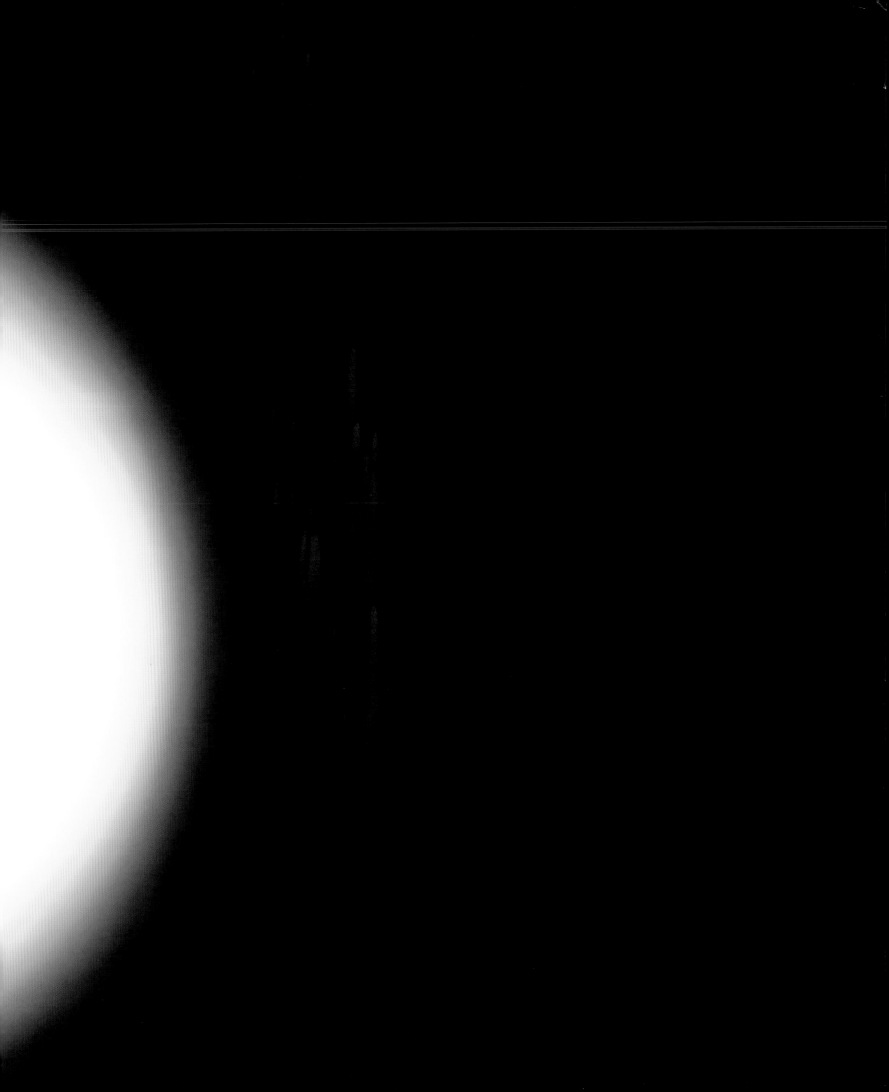

FIDEL CASTRO

PHOTO CREDITS